AUSTRALIA

BY SUE BRADFORD EDWARDS

Essential Library

An Imprint of Abdo Publishing
abdobooks.com

ABDOBOOKS.COM

Published by Abdo Publishing, a division of ABDO, PO Box 398166, Minneapolis, Minnesota 55439. Copyright © 2023 by Abdo Consulting Group, Inc. International copyrights reserved in all countries. No part of this book may be reproduced in any form without written permission from the publisher. Essential Library™ is a trademark and logo of Abdo Publishing.

Printed in the United States of America, North Mankato, Minnesota.
102022
012023

Editor: Priscilla An
Series Designer: Maggie Villaume

Library of Congress Control Number: 2022940124

PUBLISHER'S CATALOGING-IN-PUBLICATION DATA

Names: Edwards, Sue Bradford, author.
Title: Australia / by Sue Bradford Edwards
Description: Minneapolis, Minnesota: Abdo Publishing, 2023 | Series: Essential Library of Countries | Includes online resources and index.
Identifiers: ISBN 9781532199363 (lib. bdg.) | ISBN 9781098274566 (ebook)
Subjects: LCSH: Australia--Juvenile literature. | Islands of the Pacific--Juvenile literature. | Australia--History--Juvenile literature. | Geography--Juvenile literature.
Classification: DDC 994--dc23

CONTENTS

A TOUR OF AUSTRALIA

Jacob yawned and stretched his cramped arms and legs. He and his parents had just arrived at the Sydney Airport in Australia. They had left Los Angeles, California, 15 hours ago. He had barely slept on the flight, as he was rereading the Australian tour book he had bought a couple of months before. As his family stepped out of the doors of the airport, the sun was just peeking over the horizon. Jacob couldn't wait to start exploring.

Approximately 8.6 million tourists visited Australia in 2019.[1]

The Sydney Harbor Bridge connects the suburbs in the North Shore with the central business district.

Sydney's Saint James station was one of the first underground railway stations in Australia.

"I'm starving," his dad said, putting his arms around Jacob and his mom. "Let's get some food before we go to Saint Mary's Cathedral and the Opera House. We have a lot to do before our next flight to Port Douglas."

Their family took the train into Sydney and disembarked at Saint James Station. After exiting the underground station, they located a nearby café where they easily got a table. A smiling waitress brought the flat white coffees they ordered. They placed their orders for breakfast, or "brekkie," as the Australians called it. Soon three mouth-watering meals were on their table.

Jacob's dad took a large bite out of his smashed avocado and Vegemite on toast. His mom was eating ricotta hotcakes decorated with berries and a pinch of powdered sugar. Jacob had ordered the Aussie fry-up, which his tour book said was a popular Australian breakfast. It included fried eggs, bacon, sliced mushrooms and tomatoes, and beans. His stomach rumbling in hunger, Jacob quickly dug in and soon polished off his plate. Satisfied with their delicious breakfasts, Jacob and his parents headed out to spend several hours exploring Sydney.

SIGHTSEEING IN SYDNEY

Jacob's family strolled through Hyde Park. Created in 1792, it was a vast green expanse in the middle of the bustling city center. People wandered along wide walkways lined with enormous trees, and there were a few groups of people having picnics on the green grass. Flower beds, fountains, and a large rectangular reflecting pool stretched beneath

SIMILAR BUT DIFFERENT

In many ways, Australian culture is like American culture, but there are differences. Many foods look like American foods but vary based on local ingredients. Instead of having oats, almonds, sunflower seeds, and raisins, granola will have oats, wattle seeds, macadamia nuts, and bush berries. Breakfast sausage looks similar but may be made with emu meat instead of pork. Vegemite, a black spread made of yeast, has no American equivalent.

the sunny blue sky. Jacob's family enjoyed the shade of massive Hill's weeping figs that lined the walkways before they arrived at the cathedral.

Jacob's mother, an architect, was eager to see Saint Mary's Cathedral. She said that although it looked very European, it was made from local stone and included Australian plants in its many carvings. The entrance stood beneath a massive, round rose window and between two sandstone towers. No religious service was in progress, so they quietly entered the largest sanctuary that Jacob had ever seen. The buttressed ceiling soared 73.8 feet (22.5 m) overhead.[2] The stained-glass windows glowed, the multicolored light creating patterns on the wooden floor.

Back outside, they continued walking and eventually reached the harbor. Jacob immediately recognized the sail-shaped scoops that made up the roof of a building he'd seen in movies. The Opera House, another iconic piece of architecture, has been part of Sydney since 1973. They took photos of themselves with the structure in the background. Then they did the same thing with the Sydney Harbor Bridge. Jacob squinted into the distance, surprised to see cyclists and pedestrians using the same bridge as cars and an approaching train.

It was well past noon when they stopped at a pub where the menu included fish-and-chips, meat pies, and burgers. Jacob's burger had the familiar beef patty and cheese but also included beets, a classic Australian burger topping. After eating, they took the train back to the airport. As Jacob and his parents were waiting for their plane to land, Jacob wandered into a gift shop and bought a chocolate bar called Cherry Ripe. It was deliciously rich, and the cherry flavors

Saint Mary's Cathedral is built in the style of Gothic architecture. The Gothic style is characterized by pointed arches, flying buttresses, and stained-glass windows.

meshed well with a strong taste of coconut. The sweetness of the chocolate bar energized him for the next part of their trip.

DAINTREE NATIONAL PARK

The flight to Port Douglas in the state of Queensland took just over three hours. After the previous night's flight and the extensive walking they had done, Jacob was relieved to disembark the plane. They picked up their rental car so they could head to their hotel.

In the morning, the family grabbed breakfast in the dining room and then drove to Mossman Gorge, part of the Daintree National Park, which was on the land of the Eastern Kuku Yalanji Aboriginal people. Jacob's mother had chosen a Dreamtime Walk for the family so they would experience the land as it was understood by its original inhabitants. Jacob liked that idea,

Situated near the Great Barrier Reef, Port Douglas is a popular tourist destination.

especially after he had studied the park website. He and his parents were athletic, but they had never hiked in Australia. Multiple warnings were posted throughout the website about slippery conditions, dangerous falls, crocodiles, and cassowaries. Staying away from the water seemed like a good way to avoid crocodiles, but Jacob was less certain about cassowaries. He knew these large birds lived in the forest but wasn't sure if he might encounter them in the gorge or on the mountains, so exploring with an experienced guide was ideal.

After parking their car, everyone put on insect repellent and checked their packs for the drinking water they always carried. They also brought rain ponchos since they were entering a rain forest. Large greenery and towering trees with fanlike leaves welcomed them into the ancient forest. As they followed their guide, one of the Kuku Yalanji people who led visitors through the forest, the man stopped periodically and pointed out plants used by his people. The crushed leaves of the soap bush yielded a rich, sudsy lather while the tall blue quandong tree provided shade for smaller plants and, at certain times of the year, grew an

CROCODILE DANGER

The Daintree National Forest is in Queensland, a state where crocodiles make their homes. Visitors to the park are warned that knee-deep water can hide a large reptile and that nowhere within 16.4 feet (5 m) of the water's edge is entirely safe, because crocodiles hunt along the edge of the water, especially at dusk and dawn.[3] People who are traveling with dogs are warned that their pets might attract these large predators and should be kept on a leash and away from the water.

edible dark-blue fruit. As the guide talked, a little boy in their group reached out his hand to touch some harmless-looking leaves. But the guide shouted in warning. The heart-shaped leaves of the stinging tree were covered in tiny venomous hairs that would leave a painful injury if touched. Afterward at the lodge, they saw announcements for a barbeque. The menu included burgers and snags, which were described as pork or beef sausages. While his parents were enjoying a prawn-cocktail appetizer, Jacob snagged both a burger and a snag.

THE GREAT BARRIER REEF

In the morning, the family drove to the harbor to catch the motorboat that would take them out to the Great Barrier Reef. Jacob gathered with other passengers to gaze through the boat's glass bottom. He saw skates, other fish, and tan corals. As they traveled, the colorful fish, including blue tang surgeonfish, parrotfish, and blackback butterflyfish, grew more abundant and swam in swirling masses above the coral that now included patches of red and purple.

"This is so much prettier than the reef near shore," said a woman.

"Unfortunately, the inner reef gets too many visitors," said a guide. "That puts a strain on the coral, and it isn't as healthy as the reef farther out. Healthy coral is more colorful."

Soon the boat's passengers were fitted with the gear they would need to snorkel. The boat stopped, and everyone jumped into the clear water. Jacob plunged his whole face into the water. He peered through his goggles and noticed the corals' filaments, thin white strands waving in the ebb and flow of the ocean water. Blue starfish were perched on the coral, and he recognized

The Great Barrier Reef is home to more than 2,900 individual reefs and 900 islands.

the angelfish and clown fish swimming past him. Jacob paused and watched a giant clam with iridescent blue and green along the edge of its dull tan shell. A variety of fish swam through narrow canyons of towering coral in the far distance. A large sea turtle calmly paddled by, briefly meeting Jacob's gaze with its large eyes.

CONTINENT AND COUNTRY

Australia is both a country and a continent. It is the smallest continent, but that doesn't mean it is small. Australia is the sixth-largest country in the world, and it contains 5 percent of the world's land.[4]

Australia lies in Earth's Southern Hemisphere, or the southern half of the planet, between the Pacific and Indian Oceans. This part of the South Pacific is called Oceania and is the home of 14 countries and 43 million people.[5] The largest country in Oceania, Australia is isolated from other continents and countries and is home to plants and animals that can be found nowhere else on the planet.

Settled by ancient peoples and later immigrants from the United Kingdom and all over the world, Australia has developed a unique culture with its own history, government, sports, and society. Australians consider themselves welcoming, and they encourage visitors to come find what makes their continent and country special.

OCEANIA

Oceania is 38.6 million square miles (100 million sq km) in size. Most of the region is ocean, so it contains only 3.3 million square miles (8.5 million sq km) of land.[6] This vast area is home to 14 countries: Australia, Papua New Guinea, New Zealand, Fiji, Solomon Islands, Micronesia, Vanuatu, Samoa, Kiribati, Tonga, Marshall Islands, Palau, Tuvalu, and Nauru. A region of islands, Oceania contains a variety of ecosystems including coral reefs, mangrove swamps, forests, and even deserts. The islands themselves are varied, including low or coral islands that sit near sea level and high or volcanic islands that have built up over time.

The Torres Strait separates Australia and its closest neighbor, Papua New Guinea, and is 80 miles (130 km) wide. There are more than 200 islands in the strait.

GEOGRAPHY

Located in Oceania, Australia is a low, flat country that covers 2.97 million square miles (7.7 million sq km).[1] It is an island nation that shares no boundary with another country. The average elevation is 1,082 feet (330 m), but the varied landscape contains many biomes and ecoregions.[2] These include deserts and low-moisture shrubland where evaporation sometimes exceeds the average rainfall. Temperatures vary from daytime heat to nighttime cold because there is little cloud cover or humidity to provide insulation. Within this ecoregion in central and western Australia, plants and animals have adapted to life with very little water.

Australia has many types of landscapes. Kalbarri National Park is known for its coastal cliffs, river gorges, and rock formations.

MAP OF
AUSTRALIA

KEY:
- Capital
- City
- Point of Interest

Australia also has a Mediterranean ecoregion with warm, dry summers and cool, moist winters. This area lies along the southern coast of Australia and includes forests and shrubland. Plants that live in this ecoregion have adapted to seasonal fires. Some are able to regrow from parts called lignotubers. Others flower and produce seeds after a fire.

Australia's temperate forests lie along the eastern and southeastern coasts and on the island of Tasmania. Temperature and rainfall vary according to how far south each forest lies, but in general these forests are home to broadleaf trees with wide, flat leaves and evergreen trees such as the eucalyptus and acacia. The Daintree Rainforest is a part of this incredibly diverse ecoregion.

Temperate grasslands and shrublands have trees only along rivers and streams. This ecoregion lies between dry deserts and temperate forests throughout Queensland, New South Wales, and Victoria. Only small pockets of native eucalyptus, or gum trees, remain because the land has been converted for agriculture.

Australia's tropical and subtropical grasslands are more rainy than temperate grasslands but do not receive enough rain to support tropical forests. This ecoregion lies along the coast in northern and northeastern Australia. The rainfall in this ecoregion ranges from about 35.4 to 59 inches (90 to 150 cm) each year.[4]

Tropical and subtropical broadleaf forests are two of the smallest ecoregions in Australia. These forest remnants grow along the northeastern coast, and scientists believe they are the remains of ancient prehistoric forests from 15 million years ago. Rainfall in these forests is more than 79 inches (200 cm) annually.[5]

Another small ecoregion of Australia is composed of the montane grasslands and shrublands that can be found above elevations of 4,265 feet (1,300 m) in the southeastern mountains.[6] This ecoregion occupies less than 3 percent of the total Australian landmass, but the mountains receive 20 percent of the country's rainfall, creating a wet ecosystem that is home to amphibians, grasses, bogs, trees, and shrubs.[7]

THE GREAT DIVIDING RANGE

One of the most important Australian geographical features is the Great Dividing Range, which is also called the Eastern Highlands and the Eastern Australian Cordillera. The range consists of a series of mountains, hills, and plateaus that extend parallel to Australia's east coast. The 2,175-mile (3,500 km) range is the longest in a single country and separates the coast from the rest of the continent. In the southern part of this range is Australia's highest mountain, Mount Kosciuszko, which reaches an elevation of 7,310 feet (2,228 m).[9]

The Great Dividing Range forms Australia's largest watershed, which is the geographic area that feeds water into a river system. Several rivers originate here, including the Snowy River, the Murrumbidgee River, and the Lachlan River. Because of the rainfall and rivers, this area is Eastern Australia's main water source, providing water for drinking and for agriculture. The range provides water to major Australian cities, including Melbourne, Canberra, Sydney, and Brisbane.

MURRAY-DARLING RIVER BASIN

Part of the Great Dividing Range watershed is the Murray-Darling River Basin. It covers one-seventh of the Australian continent and includes 20 rivers, although it is named for only the Murray River and the Darling River. The river basin provides water for both drinking and agricultural needs. It supplies a flourishing agricultural area that produces 30 percent of Australia's food supply.[10] Farmers in the basin produce sheep, wool, cattle, dairy, cotton, wheat, rice, wine, fruit, and vegetables.

The Murray-Darling River Basin is an important water source and habitat. The basin has more than 30,000 wetlands and hundreds of animal species.

The basin frequently experiences drought. There have been times when both the Murray River and the Darling River completely dried up. Between 2006 and 2009, rainfall in the mountains that feed the river basin was at a historic low. Temperatures were also higher than normal, which meant that more water was lost to evaporation. Reduced rainfall and high water usage caused water levels to drop. These factors also increased salinity in the remaining water and promoted the growth of blue-green algae, harming the environmental health of the river basin.

To reverse this damage while supporting agriculture, the Australian government developed the Murray-Darling Basin Plan. Under this plan, the amount of water that can be taken from the rivers is now limited, and water-related infrastructure has been improved. Dams and other systems have been built to deliver water to communities and to the irrigation systems used by farmers. Groundwater is also being used instead of only pulling water from the rivers.

THE DESERTS

One-fifth of Australia is desert. Temperatures in Australia's deserts vary according to the season, location, and time of day. In the summer, daytime temperatures can reach as high as 122 degrees Fahrenheit (50°C) in some areas, but 104 degrees Fahrenheit (40°C) is more common.

The Simpson Desert is known for its sand dunes and deep-red sand.

In the winter, temperatures are typically 77 to 81 degrees Fahrenheit (25 to 27°C) in the northern desert and 59 degrees Fahrenheit (15°C) in the southern desert.[12]

High temperatures limit what can live in the desert, as does the lack of water. The average annual desert rainfall is less than 9.8 inches (250 mm).[13] In 1924, one location near Mulyie in Western Australia actually recorded no rainfall for that year. This was the only year on record that zero rainfall happened in a certain area in the Australian desert.

The desert isn't always dry. On average, once every eight years enough rain falls to fill Kati Thanda, which is also known by the English name of Lake Eyre. The lake is the lowest point in Australia, lying at an elevation of 49.9 feet (15.2 m) below sea level. Kati Thanda is Australia's largest salt lake, and it expands to 89.5 miles (144 km) long and 47.8 miles (77 km) wide when water is present.[14]

ULURU

Uluru is the name that the Anangu Aboriginal peoples gave to the red sandstone monolith that European settlers later named Ayers Rock. Uluru is easily visible, towering 984 feet (300 m) above the surrounding sandy red desert.[15] It is part of Uluru-Kata Tjuta National Park, encompassing Uluru and Kata Tjuta, a group of rock domes west of the monolith. This area contains prehistoric rock art, ancient sacred sites, and historic sites linked to more recent events in the lives of the Anangu people. The Anangu people manage and preserve the park, maintaining their cultural ties to the desert and the stories depicted in the rock art.

When Kati Thanda fills up with water, it attracts thousands of water birds, including pelicans, silver gulls, and gull-billed terns.

In 2016, fewer than 600,000 Australians, less than 3 percent of the population, lived in the deserts.[16] Yet Aboriginal Australians have made their homes in the desert for tens of thousands of years. Among these groups are the Spinifex people who manage their cultural and national heritage in the Great Victorian Desert. The Martu of the Pilbara region live in several communities that were mostly established in the 1980s when displaced people returned to their ancestral lands. Yuendumu is an Aboriginal town of the Warlpiri people located near Alice Springs, on the margin of the Tanami Desert. The town has a fluctuating population of about 1,000 people and has a school where most of its students speak Warlpiri.

GREAT BARRIER REEF

The Great Barrier Reef is an Australian biome that contains 10 percent of the world's coral reefs.[17] Coral are marine animals that are often mistaken for plants because of the homes they build for themselves. Coral polyps are soft animals that build and live in limestone exoskeletons. Large numbers of these limestone formations together form a reef. Coral cannot move from place to place, which makes them seem plantlike as they extend their tentacles to capture food.

About 1,625 species of fish live in the Great Barrier Reef.[18]

The Great Barrier Reef's biodiversity and range of habitats make it one of the most complex ecosystems in the world.

Australia's Great Barrier Reef is 133,000 square miles (344,400 sq km) in size.[19] The biome forms the foundations for various islands, including mangrove islands. Although mangrove trees grow on these islands, most of the land is underwater during high tide. The reef is a home for various fish species and other animals, including crocodiles and turtles.

Even though the reef is built largely of limestone, it is a fragile ecosystem. It can be damaged if the surrounding ocean becomes too acidic or polluted, which can happen when agricultural fertilizer washes into the ocean. Boats and boat anchors damage the coral, as do collectors who take coral to sell in gift shops. Tourists who visit the reef can protect it by not touching the coral and by wearing reef-safe sunscreen that doesn't contain harmful chemicals.

CHAPTER THREE

PLANTS AND ANIMALS

More than 180 million years ago, Australia was part of an ancient landmass called Gondwana. This supercontinent included modern Australia, Antarctica, Africa, South America, and India. As Earth's tectonic plates shifted, Gondwana broke apart and Australia completely separated from Antarctica. At this time, rain forest covered much of Australia, but the world's temperature was cooling. The plants and animals that thrived in Australia adapted to the cooler climate, and small pockets of the original forest remained.

The Gondwana Rainforests are located in Queensland and New South Wales and include

Australia's variety of ecosystems are home to many animal
species, such as the koala.

the Araucaria and Nothofagus, two types of trees that thrived at the time of the Gondwana supercontinent. Araucarias are a genus of gymnosperms, plants with seeds not protected by fruit. Nothofagus, or southern beech trees, are part of a genus that dominates sections of the rain forest. The Gondwana Rainforests are also home to ancient conifers, trees with needlelike leaves and seeds protected by cones. Other plants within the forest include tree ferns and buttressed trees such as the white booyong and yellow carbeen, which can grow to 180 feet (55 m).[1]

These forests are also home to ancient families of birds including lyrebirds, scrubbirds, and bowerbirds. Lyrebirds are ground dwellers that are similar in size to pheasants. Male lyrebirds have long, impressive tail feathers. Rare scrubbirds are small, brown, and shy, quietly darting into the undergrowth. Male bowerbirds build elaborate structures of stones, sticks, and other materials to attract potential mates. These trees and birds represent only a few of the unique life-forms found in Australia.

MONOTREMES AND MARSUPIALS

The system into which all life-forms are classified is called the taxonomy system. It is a way for scientists to organize plants, animals, and microbes, showing how the organisms are related. Mammals are a class. Within that class are subclasses and then orders. Monotremes are an ancient order of mammals that lay eggs but provide milk for their young. There are just five species of monotremes in the world. Two of them, the platypus and the short-beaked echidna, reside only in Australia. Both have evolved to live in their Australian ecosystems.

Platypuses live along streams, sheltering in their burrows during the day and emerging to forage at night. Waterproof fur keeps them warm as they search for food. A platypus closes its eyes when it dives, using its bill to pull insect larvae from the streambed. Its bill is equipped with electroreceptors that sense electrical impulses given off by the bodies of its prey.

Short-beaked echidnas are small animals covered in spines that protect them from predation. The echidna evolved a narrow snout and a long, mucus-covered tongue. It can consume up to 4.4 pounds (2 kg) of ants or termites in one meal.[2] The female echidna lays an egg into a pouch on her belly, sheltering the baby after it hatches.

Another group of unique Australian mammals are the marsupials, or pouched mammals. Born early in the developmental cycle, marsupial young remain safe in the mother's pouch after birth, growing and drinking milk. Marsupials evolved the epipubic bone to support this pouch.

There are three categories of Australian marsupials. Dasyurids, such as Tasmanian devils and extinct Tasmanian tigers, are carnivorous meat eaters. Peramelemorphs are omnivorous, eating plants and animals. They include small striped nocturnal bandicoots. Diprotodonts are herbivorous plant eaters and include koalas, wombats, and kangaroos.

The ancestors of the modern red kangaroo lived in trees, but around three million years ago some kangaroos moved to the ground. Kangaroos evolved hopping as an efficient way to get

Some kangaroos can be seen on Australian beaches, feeding on seaweed.

around. Compared to other methods of movement, hopping burns fewer calories, which is vital for an animal that forages in grasslands and deserts.

The modern koala evolved after the Australian continent shifted north 45 million years ago and many plants died out. Eucalyptus trees thrived, but the leaves can be toxic. Modern koalas, which first appeared in the fossil record approximately 350,000 years ago, adapted to eat this hard-to-digest food source.

Wombats are compact and burrow in grasslands and eucalyptus groves, digging with their sharp claws. They evolved a defense system consisting of four plates of cartilage and fat that cover

More than 750 species of eucalypti are native to Australia.

their posteriors. A wombat can use its body to barricade the entrance to its burrow without being pulled out or harmed.

EUCALYPTUS AND ACACIA

Two of the most well-known native Australian plants are the eucalyptus and acacia. Eucalypti, or gum trees, are evergreens that do not shed their leaves. They are found throughout Australia, with different species forming forests and shrublands in every environment, except for the arid desert. Short, twisted snow gums grow in the mountains, and mountain ash and karri ash trees tower in wet forests. Eucalypti are well suited to droughts and fire, evolving to resprout from buds found beneath the tree's bark or from underground lignotubers.

Nearly 1,000 species of acacia grow in Australia, where they are known as wattle.[4]

Some species have long, narrow leaves while others have feathery groupings of tiny leaves. Because of this variety, it can be difficult to recognize an acacia tree based only on its leaves.

An acacia is easily recognizable by its flowers. Many tiny blossoms are clustered together in a ball shape or a rod shape. When the blossoms cluster in ball shapes, there can be one or many depending on the species of acacia. Australia's national flower is the golden wattle, which has numerous ball-shaped globes clustered like a bouquet.

BIRDS

Perhaps the most well-known Australian bird is the laughing kookaburra. The bird's call starts as a hiccup, becoming a loud warbling sound similar to a laugh. The sound is the flock's way of marking its territory. Kookaburras are carnivorous, eating mice, snakes, other birds, small reptiles, and yabbies, which are Australian crayfish.

Australia has approximately 830 bird species. About 45 percent of these are endemic species, meaning they aren't found anywhere else in the world.[5]

Other Australian birds are related to species that live elsewhere. This includes Australian parrots. Red king parrots make their homes along Australia's eastern coast. They thrive in the cities, where bird lovers set up feeding stations for the large birds.

Some Australian birds are commonly seen because they are sold as pets. These include the sulphur-crested cockatoo, which has a white body and yellow crest, and the budgerigar.

The emu is native to Australia and is the country's largest native bird. Emus can sprint up to 30 miles per hour (48 kmh).

Wild budgerigars, also called budgies or parakeets, are naturally green and yellow. In captivity they have been bred in colors including blue, mauve, and white.

Australia is also home to two large flightless birds, the emu and the cassowary. The emu stands from 5.3 to 6.2 feet (1.6 to 1.9 m) tall.[6] The bodies of adult birds are covered with shaggy gray-brown feathers that conceal their small wings. Emus reside throughout Australia and are unique because the male bird guards the nest and takes care of the young. Emus are raised commercially for their meat.

The southern cassowary lives in Queensland's rain forests and stands 4.9 to 6.6 feet (1.5 to 2 m) tall.[7] The bird's body is covered by long, hairlike black feathers. If approached, the birds often retreat into the forest, although a bird with young may attack. The bird has a sharp claw on each foot and a dangerous kick.

REPTILES

Australia is home to 14 percent of the world's reptile population, including both venomous and nonvenomous snakes.[8] Among the most unique varieties are the blind snakes that live in southeastern Australia. Often mistaken for earthworms, these small, slender snakes burrow and feed on termites and ants. They smell their prey with their tongues, and their eyes are small black dots beneath the scales on their heads.

Among the venomous snakes is the common death adder. Grayish brown with irregular stripes and a triangular head, it blends with ground cover in the forests, grasslands, and heaths of its coastal Australian habitats. It lures prey, including frogs, lizards, and birds, by wiggling the tip of its tail so it resembles a grub. This snake's bite can be fatal to humans if antivenom is not administered quickly.

The Australian crocodile, or saltwater crocodile, is the world's largest reptile. The average adult ranges from 9.8 to 16.4 feet (3 to 5 m) in length.[9] These crocodiles reside in rivers, swamps, and lagoons in northern coastal areas. They are largely nocturnal and opportunistic feeders that will eat anything they can catch, including other crocodiles.

Five families of lizards live in Australia, including a large monitor lizard known as a goanna. Goannas make their homes in the arid and semiarid Australian desert, hiding in rock crevices and burrows to remain safe from the heat. Dragons are small lizards with spiky scales around their heads. They include bearded dragons, ring-tailed dragons, and painted dragons. The most abundant desert lizards are the skinks, such as the blue-tongued skink and the shiny sand-swimmer. Geckos evolved to escape from predators—if a gecko's tail is grabbed, it falls off. Many geckos are spotted or blotchy to blend in with their surroundings.

MARINE LIFE

Because Australia is surrounded by ocean, it is home to a variety of marine animals including seals, whales, sharks, sea dragons, rays, starfish, and tropical reef fish such as the blue tang. Hermit crabs, like those found in pet stores, live in the wild. There are also aquatic mammals including dugongs and dolphins.

There are 15 species of dolphins that live in Australian waters. The bottlenose dolphin is gray with a white belly, a large dorsal fin, and a short, rounded snout. This dolphin can be seen swimming alongside surfers in Sydney Harbor. Both short- and long-beaked common dolphins dine on squid and small fish off the east, south, and west coasts of Australia. Using a cooperative

Bottlenose dolphins tend to live in groups, or pods. Pods contain five to 20 dolphins.

feeding strategy, they drive prey to the surface for easier feeding. The striped dolphin is smaller, with a bold black stripe down the length of its back and slender stripes along the body. They live in groups of 100 to 500 and can be seen performing aerial flips.[10]

The dugong is a huge aquatic mammal that lives in shallow bays and estuaries, a type of wetland. The gray-brown animal looks similar in appearance to a manatee. It has no dorsal fin and a flat, rounded tail fin. Two paddle-like flippers propel it slowly through the water as it looks for seagrasses to eat. Although they are listed as vulnerable in other parts of the world, these animals are abundant in Australia.

Australian wildlife faces several threats. Habitat loss and rising temperatures can leave wildlife without a suitable ecosystem, and invasive species are also a threat. Among the worst are the microbes that cause various diseases in plants, including root rot and myrtle rust, and chytrid fungus, which attacks frogs.

Yet another danger is posed by wildfires such as those that burned from October 2019 through January 2020. The fires killed or displaced an estimated three billion animals. These fires are a result of climate change and also fuel greater climate change because of the carbon dioxide the fires release into the atmosphere.

VESSEL STRIKE

Vessel strike is the term used when a boat hits an aquatic animal. Animals that spend time near the surface, including whales, dolphins, marine turtles, and dugongs, are at risk. It is unclear how often animals are hit by either small boats or large ships. Conservationists know the strikes occur because they find animals with scars from boat propellers.

STEVE IRWIN

Steve Irwin was a conservationist and television personality who shared his love of wildlife with others. Irwin grew up helping his parents capture and relocate animals in their reptile park. In 1991, Irwin met his wife, Terri. The couple starred in *The Crocodile Hunter*, their popular wildlife documentary series that emphasized the importance of protecting all endangered species.

In 2006, Irwin was filming at the Great Barrier Reef when he swam over a bull stingray. The animal struck Irwin with its stinger, hitting him in the chest. The venom caused Irwin to go into cardiac arrest, and he passed away less than an hour later. His family continues his work.

Steve Irwin's popularity reached international heights with his show, *The Crocodile Hunter*.

CHAPTER FOUR

HISTORY

The first people to settle Australia came by sea from Southeast Asia when an Ice Age lowered sea levels approximately 50,000 years ago. This reduced the passage between Australia and neighboring islands to as little as 56 miles (90 km).[1] These new arrivals were hunter-gatherers who lived off the land. They left evidence discovered by today's archaeologists. The oldest reliable date archaeologists have found for these early humans comes from the Madjedbebe rock shelter, dated at around 50,000 years old. The site is in the Northern Territory and contains rock art, stone axes, stone spear tips, and grinding tools.

Other sites show that ancient peoples took advantage of whatever foods were available.

The Australian Museum in Sydney has numerous exhibitions displaying historical and scientific objects.

Archaeologists have found the remains of fish traps and shell middens, trash heaps of shellfish shells left after ancient meals. Archaeologists also excavated burial sites including Coobool Creek and Kow Swamp. Archaeologists noted that although these ancient people, who lived 9,000 to 14,000 years ago, were taller than modern Aboriginal people, skeletal similarities show a definite connection. This provides evidence that the ancestors of today's Aboriginal peoples have lived in Australia for thousands of years.

Aboriginal peoples believe that a group of deities created the world during Dreamtime. Dreamtime explains how all life was created by the actions of supernatural spirits. It became the foundation for Aboriginal customs, rituals, and ceremonies. Rock art was a significant part of Aboriginal culture. Although the exact purposes are unknown, scientists have assumed that rock art was used to tell cultural and spiritual narratives.

PREHISTORIC PIGMENTS

Aboriginal peoples made rock art by either chipping their designs into the stone or painting the surface of the stone. Common paint colors included red, orange, yellow, and white, all made from natural materials. Ochre is a natural mixture of clay and iron oxide. It may be red, orange, or yellow, depending on where it is dug. White pigment came from the minerals huntite, kaolinite, gypsum, or calcite. To make paint, minerals were mixed with water, saliva, blood, wax, or plant resins. Colors could also be altered by heating the minerals.

Oral tradition was another way of artistic and cultural expression. Songs were sung or chanted. Clapping sticks, boomerangs, and the didgeridoo, a long wooden wind instrument, were used to make songs. These instruments were specific to different locations.

PENAL COLONY

In 1606, Dutch explorer Willem Janszoon landed on the western side of today's Cape York Peninsula in Queensland. He mapped 186 miles (300 km) of the western coastline, and later Dutch explorers continued to visit the northern, western, and southern coasts.[2] In 1770, British explorer James Cook landed on the eastern coast. He carried maps derived from the Dutch maps and claimed eastern Australia for Great Britain, naming it New South Wales.

Willem Janszoon was the captain of the first European ship that reached Australia.

Britain had been transporting convicts to the American colonies, but that was no longer possible because of the American Revolution (1775–1783). Instead, Britain decided to establish a new penal colony in New South Wales. In January 1778, Admiral Arthur Phillip of the Royal Navy arrived with 11 ships carrying 1,400 convicts, navy personnel, and their dependents.[3] By January 26, Phillip had organized people to build a settlement, including farms, but much of the seed had been ruined in transport. There were few skilled farmers among the convicts, so food was soon in short supply. Phillip put both convicts and navy personnel on reduced rations. Decisions like these were unpopular with the ships' crews, but Phillip is credited with the survival of the colony.

With serious crimes such as murder punishable by execution, few convicts sent to New South Wales were hardened criminals. Britain's capital, London, was a crowded city full of impoverished, hungry people. Many criminals, including children, were sentenced for stealing food. Others were political prisoners—people those in power saw as troublemakers and wanted to get rid of. Still others had been wrongfully accused. In 1790, the Second Fleet arrived, consisting of two supply ships and four ships carrying about 1,250 male and 230 female convicts.[4] Many of those who survived the journey settled into colonial life. Once their terms of forced labor were over, many became law-abiding citizens, eager for a clean start.

> **From 1788 to 1868, the British transported more than 162,000 convicts to Australia.[5]**

At first these immigrants had fairly good relations with the local Eora Aboriginal tribe. But as more prisoners arrived and additional settlements were established, more and more Indigenous people lost their land. At least 270 massacres of Aboriginal people took place.[6] In addition, the colonists brought diseases that the local people were not immune to. Smallpox and tuberculosis were especially deadly. Although the arrival of British settlers is described as colonization, it was a cultural and physical genocide that included a destruction of Aboriginal cultural identity and the killing of Aboriginal and Torres Strait Islander peoples by soldiers, police, and even settlers.

To keep France from settling Western Australia, Great Britain established a military outpost at Swan River in 1826. Three years later, immigrants arrived in the area. Unlike the eastern states of Australia, Western Australia's colonial inhabitants were not prisoners but immigrants eager for the opportunity to buy land and build a new life.

GOLD!

In 1841, Reverend William Branwhite Clarke, an early geologist who studied the rocks and minerals of

SMALLPOX

Smallpox arrived in Sydney in 1789 and decimated the Indigenous population because of their lack of immunity to the European virus. Symptoms manifested two days after infection. They included fever, headache, backache, and a rash of rounded pustules, or pus-filled swellings. Many died within two days, and survivors were left badly scarred. The British settlers didn't know the disease was in Sydney until dead Aboriginal people were found on beaches and in caves. Up to 70 percent of the Indigenous population was killed, leaving many communities without elders and leaders.[7] There is still no cure, but a smallpox vaccine was developed in 1796.

Australia, found flecks of gold in the Blue Mountains. New South Wales governor George Gipps told Clarke to keep it a secret so convicts wouldn't seize the gold for themselves. The British government didn't investigate, and in 1848 gold was discovered in the US state of California. When thousands of men left Australia seeking California gold, the British government offered a reward for whoever discovered commercially usable gold in Australia.

Edward Hargraves was an explorer and adventurer who had tried to make his fortune in California's gold rush. He didn't find gold there but returned to Australia determined to get the reward. He recruited several local men, and they found gold in central New South Wales, which led to a story about the discovery in the *Sydney Herald* newspaper. By May 15, 1851, hundreds of people had flocked to the area, and the first Australian gold rush began.

Within the year, gold was also discovered in the Australian colony of Victoria. In 1852, deposits were found in Tasmania. More were found in Queensland in 1857 and in the Northern Territory in 1871. Eager to get rich, immigrants poured into the country, and the population quadrupled in 20 years from 430,000 to 1.7 million people.[8] The largest group of non-European immigrants was Chinese, with approximately 20,000 working in Victoria. These immigrants shifted the national identity from penal colony to one of prosperity as more and more people arrived with new ideas about how things should be.

Between 1851 and 1871, gold brought about 1.2 million immigrants to Australia.[9]

THE COMMONWEALTH OF AUSTRALIA

Each of Britain's six Australian colonies had its own government and a formal relationship with the United Kingdom. Although the colonies had common problems, such as dealing with the increased number of immigrants and railroad construction, they had no official relationship with each other.

Many Australians believed the best way to manage Australia would be an independent and united Australia. In 1880, the Australia Native Association, made up of white men born in Australia, formed to work toward nationhood. Each colony sent delegates to constitutional conventions to write a constitution describing how Australia would be governed. This constitution was approved by Australian voters, and on July 5, 1900, the British Parliament passed the Commonwealth of Australia Constitution Act 1900. Four days later, Queen Victoria declared that the Commonwealth of Australia would separate from the United Kingdom on January 1, 1901.

The new nation consisted of six former colonies turned states: New South Wales, Queensland, Victoria, South Australia, Western Australia, and Tasmania. There are also two territories, the Northern Territory and the Australian Capital Territory. Each state had its own government and laws, developed in the colonial period. However, because the Northern Territory had not been a colony and had no government, it relied instead on the laws and policies of the federal government.

Independent Australia's economy focused on agriculture, especially wool and cattle ranching, with wool production reaching a new high in the

early 1900s. Manufacturing grew, but most of
it was small-scale and focused on processing
Australia's agricultural goods.

Australia governed itself, but as part of the
British Commonwealth, the United Kingdom
controlled how it interacted with the larger
world. During World War I (1914–1918), Australia
had a population of less than five million,
and it provided the United Kingdom with
416,809 volunteers to serve in the military.[10]
These soldiers pushed Germany from its
South Pacific colonies and drove Turkey to
surrender in the Middle East. In World War II
(1939–1945), the United Kingdom's declaration
of war against Germany in 1939 served as
Australia's declaration as well. After the United
States declared war on Japan in 1941, Australia
followed suit and aided in the defeat of Japan.
The town of Darwin was damaged during 96
aerial attacks by the Japanese.

About a million Australian soldiers fought
in World War II.

AUSTRALIA'S CHANGING FACE

The Immigration Restriction Act had been passed in 1901 and codified the white Australia policy, keeping Australia for white Australians. This legislation was a reaction to non-white immigration during and after the gold rushes. Throughout the first half of the 1900s, Australian immigration policies focused on bringing people from the United Kingdom. After World War II, white Europeans from the Baltic region were allowed to enter the country. It wasn't until 1966 that the law was altered to remove barriers for non-Europeans to immigrate into Australia, although there were still more restrictions for refugees.

As Australian cities expanded and more land was developed, many Australians worried about preserving the natural and historic beauty of their country. Kelly's Bush was a natural area near Sydney that had been donated as a public green space that also housed sandstone carvings of the Wallumedegal people, an Aboriginal tribe. When the land was sold to be developed into luxury homes, the Builders Labourers' Federation (BLF) protested with local organizers. This 1971 effort to preserve Kelly's Bush was the first environmental ban, called a green ban. With the BLF's participation, no building could take place and the ban succeeded. Many similar initiatives have preserved important cultural areas like Budj Bim in Victoria.

Budj Bim is a large aquaculture site where the Gunditjmara people built stone dams, channels, and weirs, walls that crossed streams, to capture eels, fish, and turtles for food. More than 6,600 years old, it is the world's largest and oldest fish farming site. In 2019, it became the first Australian site added to the United Nations Educational, Scientific and Cultural Organization (UNESCO) world

heritage list for its Aboriginal cultural significance. Australians struggled with how to preserve their heritage as they moved forward.

One step in this forward progress was admitting past wrongdoings. On February 13, 2008, Prime Minister Kevin Rudd gave an apology to Australia's Aboriginal people. Rudd admitted that Australian law and policy led to grief, suffering, and loss for the Stolen Generations— Aboriginal peoples who had been taken from their families and their cultures. Through this apology, Australia's Parliament admitted the part played by the Australian government.

CHAPTER FIVE

PEOPLE AND CULTURE

In 2022, Australia had a population of approximately 26 million people concentrated along the coast. It is the most populous country in Oceania, but its population density is relatively low at only seven people per square mile (2.7 people per sq km).[1] In comparison, the population density in neighboring New Zealand is 47 people per square mile (18 people per sq km), and Indonesia has 391 people per square mile (151 people per sq km).[2]

In Australia, five cities have populations of more than one million people. The two most populous are Sydney with about 5.3 million and Melbourne with about five million. Brisbane has an estimated

Torres Strait Islander peoples, along with other Aboriginal peoples, are considered the first inhabitants of Australia.

population of 2.5 million; Perth 2.1 million; and Adelaide 1.3 million. Australia's capital, Canberra, has an estimated population of about 430,000.[3]

WHERE DID THEY COME FROM?

When taking the 2016 Australian Census, people were asked to identify their ancestry. Of those who responded, 33.5 percent claimed Australian ancestry, 36.1 percent claimed English ancestry, 11 percent claimed Irish ancestry, 9.3 percent claimed Scottish ancestry, and 5.6 percent claimed Chinese ancestry.[4]

Despite this level of European identification, Australia is considered a diverse society. The 2016 Census showed that 33 percent of Australians had been born overseas. The countries that contribute the most immigrants are the United Kingdom, New Zealand, China, and India.

Approximately 2.8 percent of the Australian population is Aboriginal or Torres Strait Islander.[5] Torres Strait Islanders live on a scattered group of islands located in the Torres Strait, north of mainland Australia. The northernmost of these islands is only 2.5 miles (4 km) from the neighboring

country of Papua New Guinea. In 2015, approximately 6,800 Torres Strait Islanders were living on the islands and 42,000 were living on the continent, mostly in Queensland.[7] They are Melanesian in origin and indigenous to Australia but unrelated to the Aboriginal peoples. Melanesia is an Oceania subregion including Papua New Guinea, Tonga, Fiji, Vanuatu, and the Solomon Islands.

Aboriginal Australians were the first people to live on the continent, hunting and gathering throughout the countryside. At one point there were about 500 different dialects spoken by the Aboriginal peoples. In the 2016 census, there were 64,800 people speaking an Indigenous language.[8] Many speak Kriol. Kriol is a language that was created because of colonization. As Aboriginal and Torres Strait Islander peoples were taken away from their homelands, they formed their own dialect made up of English and traditional Indigenous languages. Kriol is most commonly spoken in Western Australia and Northern Territory.

In addition to English and Indigenous languages are languages brought to Australia by recent immigrants. One-fifth of the people counted in the 2016 census said they speak English in public but another language at home. The most common language other than English is Mandarin, but growing numbers of people speak Arabic, Cantonese, and Vietnamese.

HOLIDAYS

Australians celebrate a variety of holidays including religious and patriotic days. Many of these holidays, including Christmas, Boxing Day, and Easter, are celebrated around the world. But Australians also celebrate holidays that are unique to their nation.

On January 26 of each year, Australians celebrate becoming a nation on Australia Day. This celebration started shortly after Sydney was established, but it wasn't until 1946 that the commonwealth government decided all Australians should celebrate on the same day. For many years it was a floating holiday, celebrated on the Monday closest to January 26. Since 1994, it has been celebrated on January 26 instead of on the nearest Monday. People celebrate with music, barbeques, parades, and fireworks. It is often the day that immigrants become citizens.

Canberra Day is a regional holiday celebrated on the second Monday of March in the Capital Territory, where Canberra is the only city. Canberra was founded on March 12, 1912. Australians created this new capital city instead of choosing between Sydney and Melbourne.

Anzac Day is celebrated on April 25 and is seen by many Australians as their most important holiday. Anzac stands for the Australian and New Zealand Army Corps, a combined military force that fought in World War I. The Anzac troops were part of the Allied forces, which included the United States and the United Kingdom. In 1915, Allied troops sought to capture the

Fireworks are a common display when celebrating Australia Day.

Gallipoli Peninsula in what is now known as Turkey. Then they would move on to capture the city of Constantinople, the capital of the Ottoman Empire. Allied forces, including many Anzac troops, landed at Gallipoli on April 25, and fighting went on for eight months. The Allies lost the battle, and by the time they evacuated, some 8,000 Anzac soldiers had been killed.[10] Their sacrifice is commemorated on Anzac Day.

National Reconciliation Week is celebrated by all Australians from May 27 to June 3. This week commemorates the 1967 referendum, when Aboriginal and Torres Strait Islander peoples were finally recognized in the census by an overwhelming majority vote. The last day of the holiday is a celebration of June 3, 1992, when the Australian High Court acknowledged Aboriginal and Torres Strait Islander peoples as the original owners of the land. Throughout the week, groups including workplaces, schools, and community groups

ANZAC BISCUITS

In Australia, the desserts known as cookies in the United States are called biscuits. But Anzac biscuits weren't sweet treats eaten by the Anzac troops in Gallipoli. In the army, biscuits known as ship's biscuits were rock-hard and eaten only out of necessity. A version of these biscuits made back home, called Anzac biscuits, were sold at parades, galas, and festivals, with the money raised going to support the soldiers who were fighting. Anzac biscuits were made from rolled oats, similar to but heavier than oatmeal, and versions of these biscuits are still made today for Anzac Day.

host many events to show support for reconciliation. Events can include exhibitions, presentations, film screenings, weaving workshops, and more.

RELIGIONS

The majority of Australians who identify as practicing a religion are Christian, with 43 percent of Christians being Catholic and 25 percent being Anglican.[11] With Australia's changing population, several non-Christian religions are growing in representation. Hinduism may be the fastest-growing religion in Australia because of the number of immigrants from India settling in the country, primarily in Melbourne.

Another religion that is growing in Australia is Sikhism. Most Australian Sikhs are immigrants from India. Australians got to see how Sikhs practiced their faith during the COVID-19 pandemic. The government implemented lockdowns in Australia, which meant that many people who worked with the public, including restaurant and cinema staff, received little to no income. These people, some of them university students from other countries, found that they could not both buy food and pay their rent. Sikhs believe in *seva*, or selfless service, and every Sikh temple has a soup kitchen to feed those who cannot feed themselves. These kitchens helped thousands of out-of-work Australians during the pandemic.

Islam is growing in Australia, with 2.6 percent of all Australians practicing this faith.[12] More than one-third of these people were born in Australia.[13] Muslim immigrants come from many countries, including Lebanon, Turkey, and Afghanistan. Unfortunately, in 2021, 80 percent of respondents in a national survey conducted by the Australian Broadcasting Company said that Islamophobia is a problem In Australia.[14]

Violence against Australian Muslims has also increased. On March 15, 2019, Brenton Tarrant, an Australian white supremacist, shot and killed 51 people at two New Zealand mosques. Since then, Australia's Islamophobia register, an anonymous online reporting system, has received reports on a fourfold increase in anti-Muslim hate crimes.[15] In 2019, at a café in Sydney, Rana Elasmar was physically assaulted by Stipe Lozina because she was wearing a hijab. Elasmar was 38 weeks pregnant at the time. Lozina was sentenced to three years in prison for the attack, and Elasmar now advocates for hijab-wearing women like herself.

FREE TIME

Arts and sports are popular leisure-time activities in Australia, with Australians watching and

Many Muslim Australians are working to educate people on Islamophobia.

participating in swimming, biking, soccer, basketball, tennis, and other sports. But these aren't the only sports Australians love. With the country's coastline, it is no surprise that surfing is popular, and surfers of various skill levels take to the waves at Sydney's Northern Beaches, Byron Bay, Torquay, and other destinations.

Cricket is another popular sport in Australia, from elite-level competitive play to families playing in backyards and on beaches. In competition, two teams usually play on an a oval field using flat bats and a hard, solid ball that is thrown to the batsman by the bowler. The batsman tries to hit the ball, scoring points if the ball clears the pitch or the batsman scores a run before the ball is returned.

Australian Rules Football, also known as Aussie Rules, or footy, is another popular sport. More than 1.5 million Australians play the game.[16] The rules were created in 1858, which predates the invention of American football. In the game, players kick and catch an oblong ball.

Another popular contact sport is rugby union, or rugby. The players on one team try to kick, run, and pass the ball to advance it and score points

while the other team attempts to block them. It is a contact sport in which severe injuries can occur. Younger players can take part in noncontact rugby, including a version of rugby known as Touch-7s.

Popular art ranges from dance and music to the visual arts. When European colonists came to Australia, they brought with them a tradition of landscape painting. Australia's landscapes were depicted by both Caucasian and Indigenous artists including the popular watercolorist Albert Namatjira, who often depicted the white trunks and branches of gum trees in the foreground against dramatic mountains.

In 1971, a teacher near Alice Springs encouraged the Aboriginal men he knew to paint their stories on boards and canvas. They painted the stories passed down through their families, and Australian Aboriginal art made its way into galleries and into people's homes. Aboriginal women also started to paint, and artists expanded from the colors of desert ochre to add modern paint colors, but each region still has its own style and techniques.

EVONNE GOOLAGONG

Born in New South Wales, Evonne Goolagong is a member of the Wiradjuri Aboriginal people. In 1953, her family moved to Barellan, a town southwest of Sydney, where her father got a permanent job raising sheep.

Goolagong would watch her two older siblings play tennis at the tennis courts behind the family home. Her siblings eventually taught her how to play. By 1965, Goolagong had won every title there was for her to win in New South Wales. She continued to play throughout the country and traveled to England to play at Wimbledon. The public marveled at her smooth and precise movements. Other players, including Margaret Smith Court, praised her for her unpredictable play. Goolagong played professionally until 1983. She won the singles title twice at Wimbledon, defeating greats Billie Jean King in her first win and Chris Evert in her second win.

In 2018, Goolagong was appointed Companion of the Order of Australia, the nation's highest recognition for outstanding service and achievement.

POLITICS

The structure of Australia's government is loosely based on that of the United Kingdom. It has three branches of government that are frequently referred to as arms: the executive arm, the judicial arm, and Parliament. The Australian Parliament has two houses, the House of Representatives and the Senate. The House of Representatives has 151 elected members, each representing one of the country's electorates. The House, known as the lower house, debates and votes on bills. The Senate is the upper house, composed of 76 senators with 12 elected in each state and two from each territory. The Senate reviews and approves all laws, assuring that they are fair for every state and territory.

Australian representatives debate and vote on bills in the Chamber of the House of Representatives.

Anthony Albanese became Australia's 31st prime minister in May 2022.

The executive branch is composed of the prime minister, who is the head of this branch, and the cabinet ministers. The prime minister is chosen by Parliament and is traditionally a member of the House of Representatives. There is no maximum term of service for the prime minister. As long as the prime minister is in Parliament and continues to have Parliament's support, that person can stay in office. The prime minister is the spokesperson for the government and represents Australia overseas. The prime minister leads meetings to discuss new policies and bills and leads the cabinet in determining new policy.

A cabinet minister can hold multiple positions. For example, in 2022 Marise Payne was the Minister for Foreign Affairs and the Minister for Women. She dealt with Australia's overseas policy and policies that impacted women. Ken Wyatt was the Minister for Indigenous Australians, a role devoted to improving the lives of Aboriginal Australians and Torres Strait Islander people. In 2015, he became the first Indigenous Australian member of the Federal Executive Council to advise the governor-general when he was sworn in as the Assistant Minister for Health. Other ministers and assistant ministers work in Mental Health and Suicide Prevention, Emergency Management and National Recovery and Resilience, Regional Education, Regional Communications, Public Service, Regionalization, and Industrial Relations.

In August 2018, Marise Payne became Australia's Minister for Foreign Affairs.

The judicial branch enforces the laws and is composed of three general federal courts. The Federal Circuit and Family Court was established in 2021, bringing together two separate courts. It has two divisions; one division deals with only family law matters, while the other oversees family law, migration, and other general federal law matters. The Federal Court of Australia hears economic and social cases that deal with bankruptcy, corporations, native title, taxes, trade practices, and appeals. Native title is recognition that Aboriginal and Torres Strait Islander peoples have rights concerning their ancestral lands including the right to live and build on the land, hunt and gather, and protect the land. The High Court of Australia is the final court of appeals from Federal, State, and Territory courts. It also hears federal cases that call for interpretation of the Constitution. The executive arm, Parliament, and courts are also mirrored on the state and territory level by a governor, state parliament, and state courts.

QUEEN ELIZABETH II

Queen Elizabeth II was crowned in London's Westminster Abbey in June 1953. She visited Australia from February to April 1954, becoming the first reigning monarch to set foot in Australia. As part of this celebration, a golden gown embroidered with wattle flowers was designed for her. She not only wore the dress during the tour but also had a portrait of herself painted in which she wears the easily recognizable symbol of Australia.

CONSTITUTIONAL MONARCHY

Australia is also a constitutional monarchy, meaning that a monarch who inherits the crown shares power with a constitutional government. In the case of Australia, the monarch of the United Kingdom shares power with the three arms of the Australian government. Australia is not formally part of the United Kingdom, and the monarch's role is largely symbolic and limited by the constitution.

THE ORDER OF AUSTRALIA

Queen Elizabeth II created the Order of Australia on February 14, 1975. Anyone can nominate a worthy Australian for the award. There are two divisions, General and Military, and multiple levels in each division depending on the nature of the service. People can be nominated for a wide range of categories including architectural achievement, arts, environment, helping the disabled, engineering, informational technology, media, and medicine. The appointments in the Order of Australia are typically revealed in January and June.

Australia's constitution assigns the monarch's power and duties to the governor-general, a person who is chosen by the monarch with advice from Australia's prime minister. The governor-general is Australia's head of state and performs both ceremonial and constitutional duties. The governor-general's ceremonial duties include being the Chancellor of the Order of Australia. In this position, he or she approves awards to recognize Australian citizens for their contributions to the country. The governor-general also hosts visiting leaders from around the world and recognizes and receives new ambassadors and ministers from other countries.

The governor-general's constitutional duties involve the three arms of government. The governor-general calls Parliament into session. Within the executive arm, the governor-general swears in new ministers and government officials and acts as an adviser to the various government ministers. Within the judicial arm, the governor-general appoints and dismisses judges.

Finally, the governor-general is also the commander in chief of the Australian Defense Force. The Australian Defense Force was created in 1976 to unify the three branches of the nation's military, the Australian Army, the Royal Australian Navy, and the Royal Australian Air Force. There is no mandatory military service in Australia. As the commander in chief, the governor-general commissions officers in the army, navy, and air force. This person presents flags, banners, and other honors to military units and personnel and also visits military units. Additionally, the governor-general serves as a leader during commemorative events.

POLITICAL PARTIES

Political parties play an important role in Australian politics. There are 151 members in the Australian House of Representatives. The party with the majority of seats is the ruling party and chooses the prime minister. Parties sometimes form coalitions so they can form a majority against another party.

There are three main political parties in Australia. The Australian Labor Party is the oldest and was formed in 1901. It first had the majority in 1910. Traditionally, Labor is supported by the labor unions that assist workers, advocating for higher wages and safer working conditions. Early on, Labor also worked to get property ownership removed as a qualification for voting and to make employers responsible when workers were injured in industrial accidents.

The Liberal Party was formed in opposition to the Labor Party and was formally launched in 1945. This party attracted people, including veterans who had fought in World War II, who wanted to see changes in Australia after the end of the war. The Liberal party was determinedly anti-socialist, working against Communism.

The National Party was founded in 1920 as the Country Party. It became the National Country Party in 1975 and the National Party of Australia in 1982. The organization is often known as the

Nationals. The early focus of this party was to support agriculture. Today it supports regional interests of all kinds, from agriculture to tourism.

There are several other parties in Australia, although minor parties may sometimes hold only a single seat in Parliament. These include the Green Party, known as the Greens, which focuses on environmental concerns and everyday people. Another minor party, One Nation, is led by Senator Pauline Hanson, who holds anti-Muslim and anti-immigration views.

In Australia, voting is mandatory. This means that whether an election is local, state, or federal, all citizens age 18 and older must vote or they may be fined. When Australia became independent from the United Kingdom, both men and women older than 21 could vote unless they were Indigenous Australian or of Asian or African descent. Indigenous Australians received the right to vote in 1962, and in 1973, the voting age was reduced from 21 to 18.

POLITICAL SYMBOLS

The Australian flag is a blue rectangle that combines three important symbols. In the upper left corner is the British flag known as the Union Jack, which reflects historical connections to the United Kingdom. Beneath that is the Commonwealth Star, a large white star with seven points

Almost all elections in Australia use a preferential voting system, where voters rank all or most candidates in order, with number one representing their top choice.

representing the six states and the Commonwealth. To the right are the five stars that make up the Southern Cross, a constellation that can be seen only from the southern hemisphere.

Australia's national colors of green and gold were officially recognized in 1984 and are worn by the country's athletes at the Olympics and other international competitions. These colors are the same as the country's national floral emblem, the golden wattle. One of many species of Australian

Athletes wear Australia's iconic national colors for the Olympics.

acacia, the golden wattle grows across the country, making it a symbol of unity. This plant is hardy, withstanding both drought and fire, and is thus a symbol of the strength of the Australian people. It isn't surprising that on national days of mourning, Australians are invited to wear a sprig of wattle.

Australia's national gemstone, the opal, is easily recognizable by people worldwide. In some Indigenous stories, a rainbow touched the earth, creating the colors of the opal. Among some

Indigenous groups, this gem is called "the fire of the desert." Because of this, the stone is an excellent tribute to Australia's arid landscape, where the stone is mined.

The national anthem, "Advance Australia Fair," was originally composed in 1878. Wanting to update the song, the Australian Council for the Arts held the Australian National Anthem Quest in 1973. The competition received more than 1,400 entries in the lyrics category and another 1,200 in music, but the council was disappointed in the quality of the work it received.[2] None of the entries, it felt, were as strong as the traditional Australian songs "Advance Australia Fair," "Waltzing Matilda," and "Song of Australia." The council decided that one of these three songs should be selected, so it did a poll of 60,000 Australians to see which song they preferred. "Advance Australia Fair" was selected by 51.4 percent of those who responded. "Waltzing Matilda" came in second with 19.6 percent of the vote.[3] On January 1, 2021, "Advance Australia Fair" was updated to replace the opening lines, "Australians all let us rejoice, for we are young and free," with, "Australians all let us rejoice, for we are one and free." This change reflected the spirit of unity shown by Australians during the COVID-19 pandemic.

GOD SAVE THE QUEEN

In 1984, after "Advance Australia Fair" became the national anthem, "God Save the Queen" was given the special title of Royal Anthem. It didn't replace "Advance Australia Fair" but would be played to open any event whenever a member of the royal family was present. Not to be left out entirely, "Advance Australia Fair" would be played at the end of the same event.

ECONOMICS

Australia has a wide variety of natural resources, especially mineral wealth, including coal, gold, and rare earth elements. Rare earth elements are a group of 17 metals that are used in various tech industries because of their electrical, luminescent, nuclear, and magnetic properties. They are used to build batteries, lasers, magnets, fiber-optic cables, and more. Rare earth elements can be found in every Australian state except Tasmania. Although China is the world's largest producer of these elements, the world's richest deposit is Western Australia's Mount Weld, where mining started in 2011.

One of the largest industries in Australia is based on the mining and extraction of iron ore. There are

The Super Pit in Kalgoorlie, Western Australia, is one of the country's biggest open cut gold mines. The area is also known as the Golden Mile.

two primary iron ores, hematite and magnetite. Both are used to make iron, which is then used in the production of steel. Hematite and magnetite are both mined in Western Australia; magnetite is also found in South Australia. Although magnetite has a higher concentration of iron than hematite, impurities make extraction of the iron more difficult, so hematite is easier to process.

Gold is mined in every state in Australia as well as in the Northern Territory. This gold is used in jewelry. It is also an investment for those who trust its value more than they trust government-issued currency. Because gold is an excellent conductor of electricity, it is also widely used in the electronics industry.

There are many other important minerals that are mined and exported from Australia. Bauxite, used to produce aluminum, is mined from several sites in northern and southwestern Australia. Copper, a highly malleable metal that can be easily shaped, is mined in locations throughout Australia. Australia's copper is drawn into wire and used to make electrical and plumbing components. Nickel is combined with other elements to make alloys, especially stainless steel, and is mined in Western Australia. Uranium, which is used as a fuel in nuclear reactors, is extracted from

COVID-19 globally affected hospitals and health care, one of the largest industries in Australia. In 2021, there were more than 1.8 million workers in this sector.

mines throughout Australia. Coal, a fossil fuel, is mined throughout Australia but primarily on the south and west coasts.

INDUSTRY

One of Australia's leading industries is health care, which includes social assistance. The health industry includes hospitals, doctors, dentists, and other health specialists, and in 2017 an estimated

12.6 percent of the workforce was employed in this sector.[1] Part of the reason for the importance of health care is that Australia's population is aging, and aging people often have more medical needs than younger people. COVID-19 infections also created a need for health care.

Australia's natural wonders help fuel the nation's tourist industry. Visitors come from China, Japan, Singapore, the United Kingdom, and the United States for the beaches, unique plants and animals, music, food, and wine. This industry employed approximately one million people in 2018 and also fuels the need for food workers and people to work in hotels and other accommodations.[2]

Two other significant industries in Australia are grocery stores and consumer goods. During the COVID-19 pandemic, there was growth in consumer spending. This is perhaps because Australians were not spending money on travel; instead, they were spending their money on clothing, furniture, household items, and other consumer goods. Grocery retail is considered one of the most competitive industries in Australia. Woolworths and Coles are two Australian grocery giants that face competition from two international stores, Aldi

TOP EXPORTS

With Australia's mineral wealth, it is no surprise that the country is the world's leading exporter of iron ore and coal briquettes. Coal briquettes are the form of coal that is used to heat homes. Australian agriculture provides the nation's other two major exports. Australia leads the world in the export of wool as well as sheep and goat meat. Australia exports primarily to China, Japan, South Korea, India, and the United Kingdom.

The portrait of Queen Elizabeth II is displayed on the front of the five-dollar note.

from Germany and Costco from the United States. These grocery chains compete for customers by providing online shopping and other services.

On March 3, 2022, one Australian dollar was equivalent to $0.73 in US currency.[3]

CURRENCY

Australia's national currency is the Australian dollar, abbreviated AUD, which is printed in denominations of $5, $10, $20, $50, and $100. All Australian coins are minted at the Royal Australian Mint in Canberra. The coins do not have names like penny, nickel, or dime but are named for their values. The five-cent coin has a picture of an echidna, the ten-cent coin a lyrebird, the 20-cent coin a platypus, and the 50-cent coin the Commonwealth Coat of Arms. The dollar coin has five kangaroos, and the two-dollar coin has an Aboriginal man and the Southern Cross. The one-dollar coin was first minted in 1984 and the two-dollar coin in 1988. They were introduced because coins last longer than paper money and would need to be replaced less frequently.

Because Australia had been colonized by the United Kingdom, Australia did not initially use the Australian dollar. Until February 14, 1966, Australia used British pounds, shillings, and pence. One pound equaled 20 shillings, and each shilling equaled 12 pence. This made things complicated. Still, some of Australia's leaders didn't want to change their monetary system because it was symbolic of their ties to the United Kingdom.

In the 1960s, Australia successfully transitioned to decimal currency with a dollar made up of 100 cents. The new money was designed, printed, and minted. On February 14, 1966, the new money was released. The Australian government had been preparing for the change by releasing a public relations campaign complete with animated cartoons in which Dollar Bill, a cartoon character, reassured the public that the new system was much easier. Dollar Bill demonstrated this by comparing calculations with both systems. For two years, both currencies were used while the older money was slowly removed from circulation.

TRANSPORTATION AND INFRASTRUCTURE

A variety of transportation options are available within Australia. Many Australians drive from place to place, with 92.5 percent of households having one or more cars.[4] Australia has a national system of highways that connects the state capitals as well as the cities of Cairns and Burnie. There are also state and territory highways as well as smaller roads. It is estimated that Australia has about 503,310 miles (810,000 km) of roadways.[5]

Traveling between major cities can take a lot of time because of the vast distances involved. For example, driving from Sydney on the southeast coast to Perth on the southwest coast can take 40 hours. Traveling by air is much faster, with the same journey taking only five hours. Australia has four major airlines: Jetstar, Qantas, Virgin Australia, and Tigerair.

Traveling by rail offers a way to see Australia at ground level without having to drive. There are 21,076 miles (33,919 km) of track that cross the country, providing rail transportation within

The Indian Pacific offers trips from Sydney to Perth, Adelaide to Sydney, and Perth to Adelaide.

and between cities.[7] Travelers can take one train, the Indian Pacific, from Sydney to Perth. This is a journey of 2,704 miles (4,352 km), which takes approximately three to four days.[8] Some passengers can use private rooms where they can sleep and train cars where they can load their vehicles. Another train, the Ghan, cuts across the center of Australia, carrying passengers from Darwin in the north to Adelaide in the south. The Ghan's name comes from the so-called Afghan camels and their drivers who carried supplies to Alice Springs in central Australia before the completion of the railroad. The entire journey, with multiple stops, takes more than two days to complete. It is one way to see the central desert in comfort.

With thousands of miles of coastline, it isn't surprising that another way to travel in Australia is by ferry. Ferries are large boats, often with multiple decks, that carry passengers, cars, and goods from point to point, following regular schedules and routes. Some ferry services are strictly to get from one place to another, but others are a great way to see sights and visit interesting places. Situated on a harbor, Sydney in New South Wales is serviced by several ferry lines including the Taronga Zoo ferry, which takes passengers to the zoo.

Other Australian ferries, like some of those in Brisbane, Queensland, cross rivers. Some ferry cruises are lengthy journeys. The Wallaroo ferry takes two and a half hours to travel between Wallaroo and Lucky Bay. Ferry rides can cut hours off a road trip. For example, the Queenscliff ferry carries passengers from Queenscliff to Sorrento without having to drive through Melbourne. Still other ferries are the only travel choice between certain destinations since they go where there are no roads. One example is the ferry between Cape Jervis, near Adelaide, and Kangaroo Island.

CHAPTER EIGHT

AUSTRALIA TODAY

Given Australia's extensive coastline, the ocean and beaches are a vital part of Australian life. Australia is home to an estimated 10,000 beaches, and 85 percent of Australians live within 31 miles (50 km) of a coastline.[1] During their free time, many Australians surf, fish, kayak, and picnic. People also gather to play beach cricket and beach volleyball.

They also enjoy attending sporting events and festivals of every kind, including Dancerites, the First Nations dance competition for Australia's first peoples, whether Aboriginal or Torres Strait Islander or from around the world. It is held at the Sydney Opera House.

Dancerites takes place at Tubowgule, the land where the Sydney Opera House stands today. Also called Bennelong Point, the area has long been a site for ritual celebration and dance.

Like many other events, it was postponed in 2021 due to the COVID-19 pandemic. Aboriginal and Torres Strait Islander languages, instruments, dance, and skin markings are among the cultural elements that go into Dancerites. Other popular events include the Noosa Triathlon, the Canberra Balloon Spectacular, the Melbourne International Comedy Festival, and more. Many Australians also like to attend a variety of athletic competitions, such as the Melbourne Cup horse race, the Hamilton Island sailing regatta, the World Surfing Championships, and the Formula One Rolex Australian Grand Prix.

EDUCATION

Education is a significant part of life for young Australians. They must attend school from Foundation to Year 10, which means that they go to school from age six until age 17. Students can attend either public schools, which are operated by each state, or private schools. Students attend primary school starting with Foundation, also known as kindergarten, and then Year 1 through Year 6 or 7, depending on which state or territory the student lives in. Secondary school begins in

COVID IN AUSTRALIA

Early in the COVID-19 pandemic, the Australian government decided on a policy of lockdowns and social distancing. By December 21, 2021, Australia had 260,000 total cases and 2,154 deaths.[2] But as the pandemic continued, Prime Minister Scott Morrison said that even with the COVID omicron variant surging, Australia would not go back to government lockdowns. Instead, it would rely on individual Australians to act responsibly, mask when needed, and stay home when sick. By January 23, 2022, the country's numbers had surged to 3,000 deaths and 1.5 million infections.[3] Following the peak in late March, daily reported cases once again began to fall.

Year 7 or 8, and Senior Secondary covers Years 11 and 12. After students complete Senior Secondary school and get their Senior Secondary Certificate of Education, they can go on to vocational schools, university, or full-time work. In Australia, 80.9 percent of male students and 87.8 percent of female students complete Year 12 and earn their certificate.[4]

There are eight learning areas in the Australian curriculum. English includes the study of both the English language and literature. In mathematics, students study numbers, algebra, geometry, probability, and statistics. Humanities and the social sciences cover civics and citizenship, economics and business, geography, and history. Arts education includes dance, music, drama, media arts, and visual arts. Science study includes the contributions that science makes to society and how scientific knowledge is acquired. For older students, the subject also

Most Australian primary schools require uniforms.

includes the study of chemistry, physics, biology, and earth and environmental sciences. In health and physical education, young Australians learn about the importance of leading active lives. They also study health and nutrition, and they take part in active games and sports.

The National Assessment Program–Literacy and Numeracy is a national test that is given to students in Years 3, 5, 7, and 9. The exams are taken throughout Australia in the second week of May. Students are tested in reading, writing, language skills, and numeracy, which is the ability to understand and work with numbers. Nationwide, 94 percent of students meet the minimum test score for their ages and grade levels.[5]

Students in both public and private schools in Australia wear uniforms. Boys frequently wear a button-up shirt and either shorts or trousers. In some schools, girls wear the same uniforms, but in others they must wear a skirt or dress. Some schools require all students to wear a tie and jacket.

In Australia, the school year consists of four terms, and students go to school year-round. There is a break between the end of one term and the beginning of the next, with the longest, three weeks, at Christmas. Because Australia is in the southern hemisphere, this longer break is also a summer vacation.

INDIGENOUS RIGHTS AND HEALTH

One ongoing concern throughout Australia is the health and welfare of the Aboriginal people. From 1910 to 1970, the Australian government had a policy that forcibly removed Indigenous children from their families. The idea was that the lives of the Aboriginal people would improve if they had more exposure to white Australian culture rather than their own cultures. This was because the government viewed the Aboriginal people as inferior to white Australians. Often, the Aboriginal children were sent to boarding schools where many were abused at worst or lonely and isolated at best. Many were told that their parents did not want them, and they were often poorly educated since it was generally believed that it was better to put them to work than to try to teach them. These people who were taken from their families as children are referred to as the Stolen Generations. This left a legacy of Aboriginal people who continue to experience high rates of depression, post-traumatic stress, suicide, health problems, and poverty.

In addition to mental health problems, there are medical illnesses that have been all but eliminated in the general population but continue to be a problem among Indigenous peoples living in poverty. One of these is trachoma, a bacterial eye infection that causes swelling and rolling of the eyelid. This rolling of the lid causes the eyelashes to

Gardening and growing indigenous foods provide Indigenous Australians with sources of healthy food, income, and respect for their cultures, says nurseryman Mike Quarmby, who specializes in native Australian plants. Quarmby notes that impoverished Aboriginal peoples eat far too much flour and sugar and that the foods of their ancestors would improve their health. "There are some 2,500 identified Australian native food plants," said Quarmby.[6] These foods require less water to grow than other crops because they are a good match for the environment. Possible food choices include the Murnong yam daisy, a tuber; native rice species; Warrigal green, which is like spinach; and river mint.

Many hospitals have an Aboriginal health unit that treats patients who are Aboriginal and Torres Strait Islander.

rub on and damage the surface of the eye. Repeated infections can lead to blindness. Antibiotics can treat the infection, but surgery may be required to repair the eyelid. Because the infection can be passed from person to person, it is a problem for people who live close together and do not have access to clean water and proper hygiene.

Another health problem affecting Indigenous people is rheumatic heart disease caused by rheumatic fever. Rheumatic fever is the result of a bacterial infection, most often strep or scarlet fever, that has not been treated properly. The disease develops from one to five weeks after the initial infection and is itself not contagious. As the body's immune system continues to battle the infection, it attacks and damages connective tissue in the body, causing rashes and joint and muscle pain. When it damages one or more valves in a person's heart, the person develops rheumatic heart disease.

Other health problems affect all Australians, but they affect Indigenous people at a higher level. These include mental health problems and other types of chronic illness, such as kidney disease, which affects how well the body cleans impurities from the blood, and diabetes, which affects the body's ability to produce insulin, a hormone that helps the body process glucose. Respiratory and cardiovascular diseases also occur at higher levels among Indigenous people.

The Australian government and health system are emphasizing the improvement of Indigenous peoples' health and well-being. This is being done by campaigns that discourage the use of alcohol, tobacco, and illegal substances. Additional efforts include better access to Medicare, Australia's universal health care, and medicines as well as free immunization. Although Medicare is available

Life expectancy for an Indigenous man in Australia is 71.6 years, 8.6 years less than for any other Australian man, as reported in June 2021.[7]

to all Australians, the system is complex and difficult to navigate, and services in rural areas are often limited. Government bodies are also working to improve the gaps in housing, education, health care, and employment.

ENVIRONMENTAL ISSUES

Some of the most important issues in Australia today concern damage to the environment, including deforestation. Deforestation occurs when trees are cut either for their timber or so that the land can be used to grow crops or graze livestock. When forest is cleared, land can actually become more saline or salty. Without the trees, water seeps through the soil into aquifers, porous rock that can store water. If the rock contains salt, this salt leaches out of it into the water and enters the soil. Increased salt makes the land unfit for growing crops and can also harm water quality if the salt enters runoff.

It is estimated that 13 percent of Australia's vegetation has been lost to deforestation and overgrazing since the continent was colonized.[8] This not only increases soil salinity but also reduces species diversity. Overgrazing leads to erosion and alters how water enters the soil, making it hard for plants to grow.

Deforestation can cause damage to the environment and a loss of animal habitats.

Desertification and water availability are serious problems in Australia, the second-driest continent in the world. In 2018, every state except Tasmania and Western Australia received less rainfall than normal, and record heat in Queensland led to higher-than-normal levels of evaporation. This means that the amount of water available for agriculture and household use is dropping. Australians are working to find ways to conserve and use less water.

Agriculture is responsible for 70 percent of the water used in Australia.[9] Simple changes have dramatic cuts in usage. With the aid of government funding, farmers swapped out old irrigation systems for more efficient drip irrigation. Polymer liners, called geomembranes, were added to irrigation ditches to reduce the amount of water that is absorbed into dry soil. Finally, farmers have swapped out their crops, choosing drought-tolerant varieties. Overall, these changes have cut the water used by Australian agriculture by 30 percent.[10]

Water conservation isn't just up to Australia's farmers. People who live in suburbs and cities have also found effective ways to save water. Australians have swapped out showerheads and dishwashers for more water-efficient varieties. Homeowners are also encouraged to collect

Farms in Australia are working to conserve water.

rainwater for their own use or to reuse gray water, which is water that has been used in sinks and showers.

Australia is a country that is planning for its future and working to improve the lives of its increasingly diverse citizens. This means addressing environmental concerns surrounding water and agriculture. It is also a welcoming vacation spot for visitors who travel to this island nation. With landscapes that range from lofty peaks in the Great Dividing Range to Kati Thanda in the desert and the ancient Gondwana Rainforests to the Great Barrier Reef, it is a land of unique animals and plants and a culture that is all its own.

OFFICIAL NAME: THE COMMONWEALTH OF AUSTRALIA

GEOGRAPHY

Area: 2.97 million square miles (7.7 million sq km)

Highest Elevation: Mount Kosciuszko at 7,310 feet (2,228 m)

Lowest Elevation: Kati Thanda or Lake Eyre at 49.2 feet (15 m)

PEOPLE

Population: 26.1 million (2022 est.)

Most Populous City: Sydney (4.47 million)

Ethnic Groups: English, Australian, Irish, Scottish, Chinese, Italian, Aboriginal, and Torres Strait Islander

Religions: Christianity (Protestantism, Catholicism), Islam, Buddhism, Hinduism

GOVERNMENT

Type of Government: Federal parliamentary democracy under a constitutional monarchy

Capital: Canberra

Head of State: Governor-general

Head of Government: Prime minister

Legislature: Bicameral federal parliament, with a Senate and House of Representatives

ECONOMY

Currency: Australian dollar

Major Industries: Mining, tourism, food processing, chemicals, and steel

Natural Resources: Iron ore, coal, gold, and copper

NATIONAL SYMBOLS

National Anthem: "Advance Australia Fair"

National Bird: Laughing kookaburra

National Flower: Golden wattle

G L O S S A R Y

ANTIVENOM
A serum that works against the effects of venom, a harmful and toxic substance.

BIOME
A community of plants and animals that adapt to and live in a specific climate.

BUTTRESS
An architectural feature that strengthens or provides support for a building or structure.

DEPENDENT
Someone, such as a spouse or child, who is supported by a member of the military.

DISPLACED
Describing people who were forced to leave their home or home region.

ECOREGION
An ecosystem defined by its geography and rainfall.

EXOSKELETON
An external skeleton or rigid external body covering.

GENUS
A taxonomy category below family but above species.

GROUNDWATER

Water that is naturally stored underground in caverns, cavities, and soil.

LIGNOTUBER

A woody swelling near the top of a plant's root that contains buds and food and allows a plant to regrow after fire.

MALLEABLE

Able to be hammered or pressed into a new shape.

PENAL COLONY

A place where prisoners are sent to live.

SALINITY

Saltiness or the amount of salt dissolved in something.

SKATE

A large, flat fish that has a stinger for protection.

TECTONIC PLATE

A huge piece of rock that makes up Earth's crust and upper mantle.

ADDITIONAL **RESOURCES**

SELECTED BIBLIOGRAPHY

Geggel, Laura. "Why Are There So Many Marsupials in Australia?" *Live Science*, 3 Mar. 2019, livescience.com. Accessed March 2, 2022.

Migiro, Jeffrey. "Was Australia Really Founded as a Penal Colony?" *World Atlas*, 17 Dec. 2019, worldatlas.com. Accessed March 2, 2022.

Wright, Clare. "How Women Won the Vote in Australia." *La Trobe University*, June 2017, latrobe.edu.au. Accessed March 2, 2022.

FURTHER READINGS

Pajalic, Amra, and Demet Divaroren, editors. *Growing Up Muslim in Australia*. Allen & Unwin, 2019.

Pascoe, Bruce. *Young Dark Emu, a Truer History*. Magabala Books, 2019.

Wilkinson, Carole. *Putting Australia on the Map*. Wild Dog Books, 2020.

ONLINE RESOURCES

To learn more about Australia, please visit **abdobooklinks.com** or scan this QR code. These links are routinely monitored and updated to provide the most current information available.

MORE INFORMATION

For more information on this subject, contact or visit the following organizations:

National Library of Australia
Parkes Pl.
Canberra ACT 2600
nla.gov.au
The National Library of Australia is home to the most complete collection of publications, both historic and contemporary, relating to Australia. In addition to electronic media and print, there are also museum-quality exhibits.

National Museum of Australia
Lawson Crescent
Acton Peninsula
Canberra ACT 2601
nma.gov.au
The National Museum of Australia preserves Australia's history from the First Peoples and later immigrants to the area.

CHAPTER 1. A TOUR OF AUSTRALIA

1. "Number of International Visitor Arrivals to Australia from 2010 to 2021." *Statista*, 3 Mar. 2022, statista.com. Accessed 3 Mar. 2022.

2. "St. Mary's Cathedral." *Sydney*, n.d., sydney.com.au. Accessed 4 Mar. 2022.

3. "Be Crocwise." *Queensland Government*, n.d., environment.des.qld.gov.au. Accessed 4 Mar. 2022.

4. "The Australian Continent." *Australian Government*, n.d., australia.gov.au. Accessed 4 Mar. 2022.

5. Jason Shvili. "What Is Oceania?" *World Atlas*, 12 Apr. 2021, worldatlas.com. Accessed 4 Mar. 2022.

6. "How Many Countries in Oceania?" *WorldOMeter*, n.d., worldometers.info. Accessed 4 Mar. 2022.

CHAPTER 2. GEOGRAPHY

1. "Consultation Document on Listing Eligibility." *Australian Government*, n.d., agriculture.gov.au. Accessed 1 July 2022.

2. "Elevations." *Australian Government*, n.d., ga.gov.au. Accessed 4 Mar. 2022.

3. Tim Low. "Island Nation: Australia's 8222 Islands." *Australian Geographic*, 24 Nov. 2011, australiangeographic.com.au. Accessed 8 Mar. 2022.

4. "Australia's Ecoregions." *Department of Agriculture, Water and the Environment*, 3 Oct. 2021, awe.gov.au. Accessed 1 Mar. 2022.

5. "Australia's Ecoregions."

6. "Australia's Ecoregions."

7. David Olson. "Australian Alps Montane Grasslands." *One Earth*, n.d., oneearth.org. Accessed 21 Mar. 2022.

8. "Australia." *CIA World Factbook*, 15 June 2022, cia.gov. Accessed 8 Mar. 2022.

9. John Misachi. "Great Dividing Range." *World Atlas*, 17 Sept. 2021, worldatlas.com. Accessed 1 Mar. 2022.

10. "Our Great Dividing Range." *Australian Conservation Foundation*, n.d., acf.org.au. Accessed 1 Mar. 2022.

11. "Mount Kosciuszko." *National Geographic*, n.d., nationalgeographic.org. Accessed 21 Mar. 2022.

12. Jared Richards. "Australia's 10 Deserts." *Australian Geographic*, 20 Apr. 2016, australiangeographic.com.au. Accessed 1 Mar. 2022.

13. Richards, "Australia's 10 Deserts."

14. "Kati Thanda–Lake Eyre National Park." *South Australia*, n.d., southaustralia.com. Accessed 1 Mar. 2022.

15. "Uluru-Kata Tjuta National Park." *UN World Heritage Convention*, n.d., whc.unesco.org. Accessed 1 Mar. 2022.

16. Richards, "Australia's 10 Deserts."

17. "Reef Facts." *Great Barrier Reef Marine Park Authority*, n.d., gbrmpa.gov.au. Accessed 1 Mar. 2022.

18. "Reef Facts."

19. "Reef Facts."

CHAPTER 3. PLANTS AND ANIMALS

1. "Gondwana Rainforests of Australia." *Radford University*, n.d., php.radford.edu. Accessed 9 Mar. 2022.
2. "What Is a Monotreme?" *Australian Museum*, 11 Feb. 2018, australian.museum. Accessed 9 Mar. 2022.
3. "What Is a Marsupial?" *Australian Museum*, 11 Feb. 2018, australian.museum. Accessed 11 Mar. 2022.
4. "Wattles." *Australian National Herbarium*, n.d., anbg.gov. Accessed 11 Mar. 2022.
5. "Numbers of Living Species in Australia and the World." *Department of Agriculture, Water and the Environment*, n.d., awe.gov.au. Accessed 1 Mar. 2022.
6. Walter Boles. "Emu." *Australian Museum*, 12 Oct. 2020, australian.museum. Accessed 11 Mar. 2022.
7. "Southern Cassowary." *Australian Museum*, 11 Dec. 2020, australian.museum. Accessed 11 Mar. 2022.
8. "Reptiles." *Australian Museum*, 13 July 2019, australian.museum. Accessed 11 Mar. 2022.
9. Cecilie Beatson. "Estuarian Crocodiles." *Australian Museum*, 19 Nov. 2020, australian.museum. Accessed 11 Mar. 2022.
10. "Striped Dolphin." *Australian Museum*, 4 Dec. 2020, australian.museum. Accessed 11 Mar. 2022.

CHAPTER 4. HISTORY

1. Fran Dorey. "When Did Modern Humans Get to Australia?" *Australian Museum*, 12 Sept. 2021, australian.museum. Accessed 2 Mar. 2022.
2. "Who Was the First European to Land on Australia?" *National Library of Australia*, n.d., nla.gov.au. Accessed 2 Mar. 2022.
3. Jeffrey Migiro. "Was Australia Really Founded as a Penal Colony?" *World Atlas*, 17 Dec. 2019, worldatlas.com. Accessed 2 Mar. 2022.
4. "Convicts: Bound for Australia." *State Library New South Wales*, 15 Oct. 2021, guides.sl.nsw.gov.au. Accessed 2 Mar. 2022.
5. "Convict Transportation Peaks." *National Museum of Australia*, 31 Aug. 2021, nma.gov.au. Accessed 2 Mar. 2022.
6. Nathan Sentance. "Genocide in Australia." *Australian Museum*, 26 May 2020, australian.museum. Accessed 22 Apr. 2022.
7. "Smallpox Epidemic." *National Museum of Australia*, n.d., nma.gov.au. Accessed 12 Mar. 2022.
8. "Gold Rushes." *National Museum of Australia*, n.d., nma.gov.au. Accessed 2 Mar. 2022.
9. "Gold Rushes."
10. "History of Australia." *Nations Online*, n.d., nationsonline.org. Accessed 2 Mar. 2022.

CHAPTER 5. PEOPLE AND CULTURE

1. "Australian Population 2022." *World Population Review*, n.d., worldpopulationreview.com. Accessed 2 Mar. 2022.
2. "Indonesian Population 2022." *World Population Review*, n.d., worldpopulationreview.com. Accessed 14 Mar. 2022.
3. "Australian Population 2022."
4. "Cultural Diversity in Australia." *Australian Bureau of Statistics*, 28 June 2017, abs.gov.au. Accessed 22 Apr. 2022.
5. "Cultural Diversity in Australia."
6. "Cultural Diversity in Australia."
7. "The People and History of the Torres Strait Islands." *BBC*, 24 Aug. 2015, bbc.com. Accessed 14 Mar. 2022.
8. "Diversity of Languages." *Racism No Way*, n.d., racismnoway.com. Accessed 14 Mar. 2022.
9. "Cultural Diversity in Australia."
10. "Anzac Day." *Office Holiday*, n.d., officeholidays.com. Accessed 14 Mar. 2022.
11. "Census Reveals Australia's Religious Diversity on World Religion Day." *Australian Bureau of Statistics*, 18 Jan. 2018, abs.gov.au. Accessed 1 July 2022.
12. "Australian Population 2022."
13. "Muslim Australians." *Parliament of Australia*, 6 Mar. 2007, aph.gov.au. Accessed 14 Mar. 2022.
14. Zena Chamas and Tracey Shelton. "Australian Muslim Communities Are a Lot More Diverse Than You May Have Thought." *ABC*, 19 July 2021, abc.net.au. Accessed 14 Mar. 2022.
15. Stephanie Convery. "Muslims in Australia Experienced Surge of Hate after Christchurch Massacre, Report Reveals." *Guardian*, 14 Mar. 2022, theguardian.com. Accessed 23 Apr. 2022.
16. "The Ten Most Popular Sports in Australia." *On the Go Sports*, n.d., onthegosports.com.au. Accessed 2 Mar. 2022.
17. Sally Butler. "'Art for a New Understanding': An Interview with Valerie Keenan, Manager of Girringun Aboriginal Art Centre." *Arts*, 15 July 2019, mdpi.com. Accessed 1 July 2022.

CHAPTER 6. POLITICS

1. "How Many People Voted in the Last Election?" *Parliamentary Education Office*, n.d., peo.gov.au. Accessed 2 Mar. 2022.
2. "Australian National Anthem." *Department of Prime Minister and Cabinet*, n.d., pmc.gov.au. Accessed 2 Mar. 2022.
3. "Australian National Anthem."

CHAPTER 7. ECONOMICS

1. "Healthcare and Social Assistance Our Largest Industry." *Australian Bureau of Statistics*, 23 Oct. 2017, abs.gov.au. Accessed 11 Mar. 2022.

2. Vic Lang'at. "What Are the Biggest Industries in Australia?" *World Atlas*, 5 July 2018, worldatlas.com. Accessed 21 Apr. 2022.

3. "Live Australian Dollar to Dollar Exchange Rate (AUD/USD) Today." *Exchange Rates*, 3 Mar. 2022, exchangerates.org.uk. Accessed 3 Mar. 2022.

4. "Car Statistics." *Finder*, 29 Mar. 2021, finder.com.au. Accessed 3 Mar. 2022.

5. "Australian Roads." *PIARC*, n.d., piarc.org. Accessed 17 Mar. 2022.

6. "World's Longest Highways: Australia's Highway 1." *GeoTab*, 10 May 2019, geotab.com. Accessed 3 Mar. 2022.

7. "Transportation in Australia Explained: A Complete Guide." *OZ Studies*, n.d., ozstudies.com. Accessed 10 Mar. 2022.

8. "Travelling by Train in Australia." *Man in Seat 61*, n.d., seat61.com. Accessed 17 Mar. 2022.

CHAPTER 8. AUSTRALIA TODAY

1. "Australia Facts." *Travellers Contact Point*, n.d., travellers.com.au. Accessed 24 Mar. 2022.

2. "Australia Rules Out Lockdown Despite Omicron Surge." *Reuters*, 21 Dec. 2021, reuters.com. Accessed 18 Mar. 2022.

3. Hilary Whiteman. "Australia Was a Model in How to Handle Covid. Now It's a Mess." *CNN*, 23 Jan. 2022. cnn.com. Accessed 18 Mar. 2022.

4. "The Australian Education System." *Department of Foreign Affairs and Trade*, n.d., dfat.gov.au. Accessed 18 Mar. 2022.

5. "The Australian Education System."

6. Sally Bryant. "Growing a Healthy Future with Traditional Aboriginal Foods." *ABC*, 22 June 2016, abc.net.au. Accessed 19 Mar. 2022.

7. "Deaths in Australia." *Australian Institute of Health and Welfare*, n.d., aihw.gov.au. Accessed 3 Mar. 2022.

8. "Issues with No End in Sight." *World Wildlife Fund*, n.d., wwf.panda.org. Accessed 3 Mar. 2022.

9. Jon Heggie. "Making Every Drop Count: How Australia Is Securing Its Water Future." *National Geographic*, n.d., nationalgeographic.com. Accessed 19 Mar. 2022.

10. "Water Account, Australia." *Australian Bureau of Statistics*, 20 Oct. 2021, abs.gov.au. Accessed 22 Apr. 2022.

<h1>INDEX</h1>